About Skill Builders Word Problems

by Jeanne S. Rawlins

Welcome to RBP Books' Skill Builders series. Like our Summer Bridge Activities collection, the Skill Builders series is designed to make learning both fun and rewarding.

Students often ask parents and teachers, "When am I ever going to use this?" Skill Builders Word Problems books have been developed to help students see the uses of math in the world around them. Exercises help students develop problem-solving skills in real-world situations while increasing confidence in their math skills.

Content is based on current NCTM (National Council of Teachers of Mathematics) standards and supports what teachers are currently using in their classrooms. Word Problems can be used both at school and at home to engage students in problem solving.

The sixth-grade math skills in this book include addition, subtraction, multiplication, division, graphing, fractions, measurement, area and perimeter, money values, and time. Special emphasis is given to multistep problems.

A critical thinking section includes exercises to help develop higher-order thinking skills.

Learning is more effective when approached with an element of fun and enthusiasm—just as most children approach life. That's why the Skill Builders combine entertaining and academically sound exercises with eye-catching graphics and fun themes—to make reviewing basic skills at school or home fun and effective, for both you and your budding scholars.

Table of Contents

Give Me a Call

Read through the problem to determine what it is asking, and then reread the problem and solve it.

1. A phone call costs 7 cents per minute. James calls Mike and talks for 18 minutes. Then he talks to Connie for 7 minutes. Then he talks to Bill for 5 minutes. How much will the phone calls cost James?

2. Mark has a $5.00 phone card. He wants to call and talk to Amy. How many minutes can he talk to Amy if it costs 39 cents to connect and 7 cents per minute?

3. Mom got her phone bill. It cost her $32.00 for the phone service, $8.93 for long distance, $3.21 for federal taxes, $2.08 for state taxes, $5.95 for voice mail and $5.95 for caller I.D. How much was Mom's phone bill?

4. Lyndon needs a new phone. It costs $89.95. He gets paid $563.21, and he needs to pay his bills first: rent $250.00, power $83.45, cable $36.95, food $113.24. Does he have enough to buy the phone?

Solve each problem.

1. Mark has $10.00. He collects baseball cards. Each pack of baseball cards costs $1.19. How many packs of baseball cards can Mark buy?

2. Sports Mart sold 9 basketballs and 14 footballs. If Sports Mart sells 8 times as many baseballs as footballs, how many balls were sold altogether?

3. James scored 21 points in the basketball game last night. He scored 18 points last week and 25 points the week before. What was the average number of points he scored per game?

4. James had 6 rebounds in his first game, 9 in the next, 14 in the next game, and 8 rebounds last night. What is his mean (average) number of rebounds?

4

Fresh Powder

Solve each problem.

The Slip and Slide Ski Resort charges $26.50 for an all-day ski pass. If 456 people ski on Tuesday, how much money does the resort take in that day?
This problem is asking how much. In this case we multiply to get our answer.

$26.50
x 456
$12,084.00

---

1. In November the Slip and Slide Ski Resort received 18 inches of snow. They got 38 inches in December, 3 feet in January, 20 inches in February, and 1 foot in March. What was the average snowfall per month?

2. The Slip and Slide Ski Resort wants to make a new run just for snowboarders. The run is $\frac{3}{4}$ of a mile one way. They need a lift that will go up and back. How many feet of lift do they need? (There are 5,280 feet in one mile.)

3. The Slip and Slide Ski Resort needs a chair every 3 feet for the lift in problem 2. How many chairs do they need to buy?

4. Each chair from problem 3 costs $32.99. How much will all the chairs cost?

5

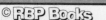

Solve each problem.

1. Lyndon has 3 boards. One board is 4 feet long, one is 27 inches long, and the other is 34 inches long. How long are the boards altogether?

2. Brent wants to put new baseboards in his den. The den is 20 feet 3 inches by 18 feet 7 inches. If the baseboards come in 4-foot lengths, how many baseboards will he need to buy?

3. The baseboards from problem 2 cost $1.09 each. How much will it cost Brent to buy the baseboards?

4. Paul is estimating the cost of remodeling. Sheetrock costs $12.00 per sheet, and he needs 9 sheets. Tile for the floor costs $.89 per tile; he needs 146 tiles. Cupboards will cost $1,746.00. Paint will be $9.99 per gallon, and he needs 4 gallons. How much will remodeling cost Paul?

The Bakery

When solving word problems, look for key words or phrases to help you know what the problem is asking for.

> **How many more than** would indicate that you **subtract**.
> **How many less** would indicate that you **subtract**.
> **Total** would indicate that you **add**.
> **Altogether** would indicate that you **add**.
> **Times**, of course, would indicate that you **multiply**.

1. Sarah wants to take cookies to a party. If there are 27 people at the party, and she wants to have at least 1 cookie per person, how many dozen cookies does Sarah need?

2. Bill's Bakery sells 327 donuts for 45 cents each. How much money does Bill's Bakery earn?

3. Bill's Bakery used 56 pounds of flour on Monday, 48 pounds on Tuesday, 51 pounds on Wednesday, 37 pounds on Thursday, 53 pounds on Friday, and 71 pounds on Saturday. How much flour did Bill's Bakery use altogether?

4. Connie is ordering éclairs for a wedding. She is planning on 575 people. If each éclair costs 29 cents, how much will the éclairs cost altogether?

© RBP Books

Word Problems Grade 6—RBP0784

Wild Animal Kingdom

Solve each problem.

The following key words and phrases usually indicate that you add:

total	in all	together
altogether	how many	

1. Last year Jenneil's Pet Palace sold 342 cats, 239 dogs, 789 birds, 1,675 fish, and 354 rabbits. How many pets did Jenneil's Pet Palace sell altogether?

2. Arwin likes to bird watch. He saw 43 robins, 112 sparrows, 7 swans, and 321 ducks. How many birds did Arwin see in all?

3. Jenneil's Pet Palace made $1,245.32 in January, $2,643.89 in February, $2,378.54 in March, and $3,159.84 in April. What is the total amount earned by Jenneil's Pet Palace?

4. Max wants to go on a safari. It will cost $1,432.94 to fly there, $542.37 for clothing, $369.54 for a new camera, $876.49 for the hotel, and $465.29 for food. How much will the safari cost Max?

Yee Haw

Sometimes we do more than one function in a problem.

Danny saw 12 horses and 69 cows on the farm. If Danny saw 8 times as many sheep as horses, how many animals did Danny see altogether?	**8 x 12 = 96 sheep** $\quad$ **12 horses** $\quad$ **69 cows** $\underline{+\ 96}$ ** sheep** $\quad$ **177 animals altogether**

1. James saw 8 horses and 123 chickens at the farm. If James saw 7 times as many cows as chickens, how many animals did James see altogether?

2. Farmer Jim has 6 times as many bales of hay as he does straw. He has 2,052 bales of hay. How many bales of straw does he have?

3. Farmer Jim sells 8 times as many eggs as gallons of milk. He sells 42 gallons of milk. How many <u>more</u> eggs than gallons of milk does he sell?

4. Farmer Jim's chickens lay 257 eggs on Monday, 148 eggs on Wednesday, and 111 eggs on Friday. How many <u>dozen</u> eggs does Farmer Jim have?

9

Tuesday was Election Day. The animals in the community voted for their favorite candidates. Use the circle graph to answer the questions below.

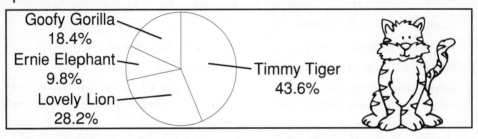

Goofy Gorilla
18.4%

Ernie Elephant
9.8%

Lovely Lion
28.2%

Timmy Tiger
43.6%

1. What was the total percentage that voted for either Goofy Gorilla or Timmy Tiger?

2. What is the percentage point difference between the candidate that received the highest number of votes and the candidate that received the least number of votes?

3. If those who voted for Goofy Gorilla had voted for Lovely Lion, would Timmy Tiger still have won the election?

4. If 1% stands for 10 voters, how many votes did Lovely Lion receive?

Tiger

Show Me the Money

Solve each problem.

The following key words and phrases usually indicate that you subtract:

how many left	**how many more than**
how many fewer than	**how many less**
how many are not	**how much left**

1. Fernando buys a watch for $34.86 and a shirt for $18.91. Sales tax is 6%. Fernando gives the clerk a one hundred-dollar bill. How much change does he get?

2. Diane spends $86.28 at the clothing store. Stevane spends $49.89 at the clothing store. How much more did Diane spend?

3. Lyndon wants to buy new ski equipment. He has $800.00. He buys skis for $386.00, boots for $92.00, a jacket for $136.00, gloves for $18.00, and ski bibs for $96.00. How much money does he have left?

4. Moshen bought a football rookie card for $23.19. Three years later he sold the card for $81.47. How much money did he make?

Le Chef

Solve each problem.

1. Carlos needs to double a recipe. The recipe calls for $3\frac{1}{2}$ cups flour, $\frac{1}{4}$ cup sugar, $\frac{1}{2}$ teaspoon salt, and $\frac{7}{8}$ teaspoon baking powder. How much of each will he need?

   Flour _____ Sugar _____

   Salt _____

   Baking Powder _____

2. Ronda makes a pepperoni pizza. She cuts it into 12 slices. If her family eats $\frac{2}{3}$ of the pizza, how many slices are left?

3. Chef Jeanne buys 5 pounds of sugar. She uses 3 pounds 5 ounces of sugar to make cakes. How much sugar does she have left? (There are 16 ounces in a pound.)

4. Jimmy's Buffet makes $236.83 on Monday. They make $329.50 on Tuesday. They make $698.43 on Saturday. How much more did Jimmy's Buffet make on Saturday than on Monday?

12

Some word problems have more information than you need to solve them. Read through the word problem to find what it is asking. Then reread the problem to find what information you need to solve it.

The Sports Mart sold 456 basketballs, 783 baseballs, and 295 footballs. How many more basketballs than footballs did they sell?

$$\begin{array}{r} {\scriptstyle 3\,1}\\ \cancel{4}56 \\ -\ 295 \\ \hline 161 \end{array}$$ **more basketballs**

---

1. The Sports Mart made $643.83 in one week. Thirty percent of this amount goes to the employees for wages. How much did the Sports Mart pay in wages that week?

2. The Sports Mart sold 389 sweatshirts, 832 T-shirts, and 457 pairs of sweatpants. How many more T-shirts than sweatshirts did they sell?

3. Sports Mart bought 58 tennis rackets and 187 baseball bats. If they bought 6 times as many baseball mitts as tennis rackets, how many pieces of equipment did they buy altogether?

4. Sports Mart has 8 times as many skis as snowboards. They have 720 skis. They have 49 more pairs of snow boots than snowboards. How many snow boots does Sports Mart have?

Ski Resort

Solve each problem.

1. If the Slip and Slide Ski Resort gets 173 inches of snow per year, what is the average monthly snowfall?

2. The Slip and Slide Ski Resort receives 173 inches of snow per year. The Slip and Slide Ski Resort gets 4 times the amount of snow that Slushy Ski Mountain gets. How much snow does Slushy Ski Mountain get?

3. At the Slip and Slide Ski Resort it snowed 6.2 inches on Tuesday, 1.3 inches on Wednesday, 12.4 inches on Friday, and 4.8 inches on Saturday. How much snow did the Slip and Slide Ski Resort receive altogether?

4. The Slushy Ski Mountain is 8,865 feet above sea level. The Slip and Slide Ski Resort is 11,042 feet above sea level. How much taller is the Slip and Slide Ski Resort than Slushy Ski Mountain?

Solve each problem. The first problem is worked for you.

The mall is 917 feet tall. The high rise is 1,468 feet tall. How many feet taller is the high rise than the mall?

1,468 (high rise)
– 917 (mall)
551 feet taller

---

1. The city library is 538 feet tall. The mall is 917 feet tall. How many feet taller is the mall than the city library?

2. The city library is 538 feet tall. The downtown high rise is 3 times taller than the city library. How tall is the downtown high rise?

3. The city library cost $1,349,739 to build. The mall cost 3 times that amount to build. How much more did the mall cost than the city library?

4. Every week, 1,492 people go to the library. Seven times as many go to the mall every week. If the average person spends $4.53 at the mall, how much money does the mall make in a week?

Ski Sale

Solve each problem.

Sports Mart Ski Sale			
Skis	$369.84	Hand Warmers	$2.93
Ski Boots	$23.50	Hats	$9.37
Gloves	$15.60	Goggles	$12.48
Snowboards	$289.37	Ski Bibs	$89.72
Coats	$138.52		

1. Marilyn buys 3 pairs of gloves, 1 coat, 7 hand warmers, and 2 hats. How much does she spend?

46.80
136.52
20.51
18.74
224.03

2. Diane spends $373.29. Margaret spends 9 times as much as Diane. How much does Margaret spend?

3,359.61

3. Chad has $500.00. He buys a snowboard, a pair of gloves, 2 hand warmers, and a pair of goggles. How much money does he have left?

289.37
15.60
5.86
12.48
500.00
323.31
176.09

4. Sports Mart sells 238 skis and 1,528 hand warmers. How much does the store make on skis and hand warmers altogether?

88,021.92
4,477.04
92,498.96

Remodeling

Solve each problem.

Rex wants to put sod in his yard. His front yard is 26 feet by 32 feet. His backyard is 20 feet by 25 feet. How many square feet of sod does Rex need to order?

32	25	832
x 26	x 20	+ 500
832	500	1,332 **square feet**

1. Claire wants to put new carpet in her house. The living room is 18 feet by 23 feet. The bedroom is 17 feet by 14 feet. The den is 15 feet by 15 feet. How many square feet of carpet does she need to order?

2. Robert is adding a room onto his house. He buys 143 2 x 4s, 28 pieces of Sheetrock, and 3 boxes of nails. The Sheetrock costs $18.76 per sheet. He spends 3 times more on 2 x 4s than Sheetrock. How much does he spend on 2 x 4s?

3. Chad's construction company bought 14,582 nails. They want to order 6 times that amount for next week. How many nails do they need to order?

4. A wall in Brandy's house is 18 feet by 24 feet. Sheetrock comes in 8-feet by 4-feet lengths. How many sheets of Sheetrock will Brandy need to cover her wall?

The Ice Cream Parlor

Solve each problem.

Ike's Ice Cream Parlor sold 387 gallons of ice cream last month. Twenty percent of the ice cream sold was strawberry ice cream. How many gallons of strawberry ice cream did Ike's Parlor sell?

$$\begin{array}{r} 387 \\ \times\ .20 \\ \hline \textbf{77.4 gallons} \end{array}$$

1. Ike's Ice Cream sold 387 gallons of ice cream last month. Forty-two percent of the ice cream sold was vanilla. How many gallons of vanilla ice cream did Ike's Ice Cream sell?

2. Ike's Ice Cream charges $1.19 for double-scoop ice cream cones. They sold 373 double-scoop ice cream cones. How much did they make on double-scoop ice cream cones?

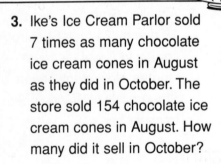

3. Ike's Ice Cream Parlor sold 7 times as many chocolate ice cream cones in August as they did in October. The store sold 154 chocolate ice cream cones in August. How many did it sell in October?

4. In the summer, Ike has 8 times as many gallons of ice cream as in the winter. If Ike has 272 gallons of ice cream in the summer, how many gallons of ice cream does he have in the winter?

Go Team

Solve each problem.

1. Coach Ingram bought
   4 times more softballs than
   volleyballs. She bought
   82 volleyballs. How many
   softballs did she buy?

2. Mike went on a trip. His flight
   took him 2 hours and
   45 minutes to get to
   California. Next week he is
   flying to New York. It will take
   him 3 times as long to get
   there. How long will it take
   Mike to get to New York?

3. James owns an apple
   orchard. He picked
   1,058 pounds of apples. If
   he puts 40 pounds in each
   bushel, how many bushels
   of apples will he have?

4. James sold 83 bushels of
   apples. If he gets $12.00 per
   bushel, how much money
   did he earn?

19

Solve each problem.

Max buys 3 bushels of peaches for $8.99 each. He buys 2 bushels of apricots for $12.00 each and 4 bushels of apples for $15.00 each. How much does Max spend?

$8.99	$12.00	$15.00	$26.97
x 3	x 2	x 4	$24.00
			+ $60.00
$26.97	$24.00	$60. 00	$110.97

1. Connie buys 29 apples for 53¢ each. She buys 18 oranges for 48¢ each. She buys 7 lemons for 24¢ each. How much does Connie spend?

2. Bill buys 7 dozen donuts at $5.99 per dozen. He buys 4 gallons of apple cider at 2 gallons for $4.50. How much does Bill spend?

3. Jeanne is making apple pies. It takes 6 apples to make a pie. If she has 143 apples, how many pies can she make?

4. Mike buys 87 apples. If he cuts them into thirds, how many slices will he have?

Baby Face

Solve each problem.

1. James uses 7 diapers per day. His family is going on a trip. They will be gone for 3 weeks. How many diapers does the family need to take for James?

2. Diapers cost $17.99 for the mega pack and $8.95 for the regular pack. If James's mom buys 4 mega packs and 7 regular packs, how much will it cost?

3. If there are 84 diapers in the mega pack, and James uses 7 diapers per day, how many mega packs of diapers will James use in a 28-day month?

4. James's mom goes to the store for baby items. She buys 17 jars of baby food at 44¢ each. She buys 3 boxes of cereal at $1.49 each. She buys 4 packages of animal crackers for 89¢ each and a new bib for $3.49. She gives the clerk $100.00. How much change will she get?

The Rawlins family ate their favorite pies for Thanksgiving.
Use the circle graph to answer the questions below.

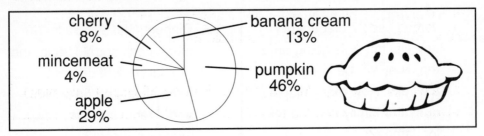

1. What percent more pumpkin pie was eaten than apple pie?

2. If the Rawlins family had eaten half as much coconut cream pie as they did apple pie, what percentage of coconut cream pie would they have eaten?

3. What is the total percentage of pumpkin, cherry, and banana cream pie?

4. Write a fraction for the percentage of cherry pie eaten.

Auto Body Shop

Solve each problem.

Brent charges $18.50 per hour to fix and paint cars. He earned $858.19 this week. How many hours did Brent work?

$858.19 ÷ 18.50 = 46.39. He worked 46.39 hours this week.

---

1. Brent charges $18.50 per hour to fix and paint cars. He earned $3,172.75 last month. How many hours did Brent work last month?

2. Brent ordered 32 gallons of paint. He painted 4 cars. The total cost of the paint was $383.68. How much did each gallon of paint cost?

3. Jimmy got his bill from the auto body shop. He owed $538.29 for labor, $43.68 for paint, $149.49 for a new fender, and $89.52 for a new tire. Jimmy paid half the bill. How much does he still owe?

4. Brent sent a bill to Carol for repairs to her car. He charged her $378.27 for labor, $29.32 for paint, $63.89 for a new mirror, and $349.29 for a windshield. He gave Carol a 10% discount. How much was Carol's bill?

Solve each problem.

1. Arwin's fruit stand opens for business in the fall. He picked 8,942 apples. If he puts 24 apples in each bag, how many full bags will he have?

2. Arwin sold 56 bushels of peaches. He sold $\frac{1}{4}$ the number of bushels of apricots as peaches. He sold 9 times as many apples as apricots. How many bushels of apples did he sell?

3. Arwin sold 110 boxes of fruit. Twenty percent of the fruit sold was oranges. How many boxes of oranges did he sell?

4. The fruit farm has 844 trees. One-fourth of the trees are apple trees. How many apple trees does the fruit farm have?

Solve each problem.

1. Jeanne has 465 rocks. She has an equal number of sedimentary, igneous, and metamorphic rocks. How many igneous and metamorphic rocks does she have altogether?

2. Jeanne loves geodes. She bought 4 geodes for $63.20. How much did she spend on average for each geode?

3. Mike's class went to the museum. The museum has 1,283 rocks on display in 8 exhibits. What is the average number of rocks in each exhibit?

4. At the museum Mike's class saw 3,503 rocks. There are 113 rocks in each room. How many rooms are in the museum?

Remember, the key to figuring out word problems is to determine what the problem is asking for.

A phone call costs 7 cents per minute. Last month Allie's phone bill was $84.63. How many minutes did Allie talk on the phone last month?

$84.63 ÷ $.07 = 1,209 minutes

---

1. A phone call costs 7 cents per minute. James's phone bill was $38.71. How many minutes did James talk on the phone?

2. Mark has $80.00. He buys a jacket for $35.89, a new bat for $18.54, and a new mitt for $24.56. How much money will Mark have left?

3. Sports Mart sold 376 balls last year. They sold 63 footballs and 189 basketballs. If the rest of the balls they sold were baseballs, how many baseballs did Sports Mart sell?

4. The Slip and Slide Ski Resort makes $256.98 each day it is open. If the resort is open 148 days this season, how much money will it make?

Solve each problem.

1. Grayson needs 154 yards of fence to go around his yard. If fence comes in 6-foot lengths, how many lengths of fence does Grayson need?

2. Paul is putting in a new sprinkling system. He buys 18 six-foot lengths of PVC pipe for $1.13 per length and 6 elbows for $.89 each. He buys 56 sprinkler heads. Twelve of the sprinkler heads cost $11.99 each, and the rest cost $2.99 each. How much did Paul spend?

3. Connie's front yard is 42 feet by 38 feet. She wants to put turf in. How many square feet of turf will she need to buy?

4. Turf costs 17¢ per square foot. Connie's backyard is 39 feet by 27 feet. How much will it cost Connie to put turf in her backyard?

Solve each problem.

Pam planted 366 flowers. One-third of the flowers were rose bushes. How many rose bushes did Pam plant?

$$366 \times \frac{1}{3} = \frac{366}{3} = 366 \div 3 = 122 \text{ rose bushes}$$

1. George planted 387 tulips, 298 petunias, 837 pansies and 1,384 roses at the Mason Mansion. How many flowers did George plant altogether?

2. Max mows lawns at the Mason Mansion. He makes $12.50 per hour. Max made $462.50 this week mowing the lawns. How many hours did Max work this week?

3. James saw 487 tulips. He saw 4 times as many roses. How many flowers did James see altogether?

4. Garden Greenhouses sold 1,892 plants. One-fourth of the plants sold were trees. How many trees did Garden Greenhouses sell?

Solve each problem.

Morgan is making chocolates for the holidays. She uses $2\frac{1}{4}$ cups of chocolate in one batch, $4\frac{1}{3}$ cups of chocolate in the second batch, and $3\frac{1}{2}$ cups in the last batch. How much chocolate does Morgan use?

Remember to convert the fractions so they have a common denominator before adding.

$$2\frac{1}{4} + 4\frac{1}{3} + 3\frac{1}{2} = 2\frac{3}{12} + 4\frac{4}{12} + 3\frac{6}{12} = 9\frac{13}{12} \text{ or } 10\frac{1}{12}$$

1. Fernando wants to make a pie. He wants to double the recipe. If the recipe asks for $4\frac{1}{4}$ cups of flour and $2\frac{1}{2}$ cups of sugar, how much flour will he need?

2. Karen buys 20 pounds of hot chocolate. She puts it in 8-ounce bags. How many bags of hot chocolate will she have? (There are 16 ounces in a pound.)

3. The bake sale made $732.82. Thirty-five percent of the money is going to the computer lab for software. How much money will the computer lab get?

4. The Slip and Slide snack bar sold 489 cups of hot chocolate in one day. Each cup cost $1.89. If they sell the same amount of hot chocolate 3 days in a row, how much money will they make?

Solve each problem.

1. Mike took a trip. His flight took 3 hours and 15 minutes to get to Seattle. Next week he is flying to London. It will take him 6 times longer to get there. How long will it take Mike to get to London?

2. Go Jet Airlines bought 325 bags of pretzels for 29¢ each. They bought 18 cases of soda pop for $8.98 per case. And they bought 23 new pillows for $3.89 each. How much did Go Jet Airlines spend?

3. Go Jet Airlines uses 2,374 gallons of fuel in one day. They need to buy enough fuel for the week. How many gallons of fuel does Go Jet Airlines need to buy?

4. Jimmy took 4 trips last month. It cost him $389.29 to fly to Oregon, $2,384 to fly to Australia, $129.24 to fly to San Diego, and $582.24 to fly to Chicago. How much did Jimmy spend on flights last month?

Solve each problem.

> Sarah wants to make soup. She only wants half of what the recipe makes. The recipe calls for $1\frac{1}{3}$ teaspoons of salt. If she wants to put in half that amount, how much salt should she put in?
>
> $$1\frac{1}{3} \times \frac{1}{2} = \frac{4}{3} \times \frac{1}{2} = \frac{4}{6} \text{ or } \frac{2}{3} \text{ of a teaspoon}$$

1. Sarah is making soup. She is making half of what the recipe makes. The recipe calls for $1\frac{1}{4}$ teaspoons of minced garlic. How much minced garlic should she put in?

2. Cassie is making cookies. She needs to triple the recipe. The recipe calls for $4\frac{1}{2}$ cups of flour. How much flour will she need?

3. Claire is making 5 cakes. It takes $2\frac{1}{3}$ cups of sugar for one cake. How many cups of sugar will Claire need to make 5 cakes?

4. Michelle is making 7 pumpkin pies. It takes $1\frac{2}{3}$ cups of pumpkin and $1\frac{1}{4}$ cups of sugar for each pie. If Michelle makes 7 pies, how much pumpkin and sugar will Michelle need altogether?

Use the graphs below to answer each question.

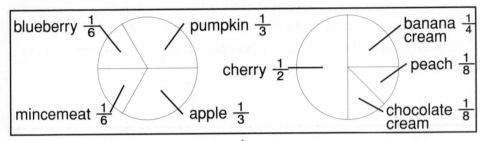

blueberry $\frac{1}{6}$ pumpkin $\frac{1}{3}$ banana cream $\frac{1}{4}$

cherry $\frac{1}{2}$ peach $\frac{1}{8}$

mincemeat $\frac{1}{6}$ apple $\frac{1}{3}$ chocolate cream $\frac{1}{8}$

---

1. How much apple, pumpkin, and banana cream pie is there altogether?

2. Which flavor of pie is there the most of?

3. How much more apple pie is there than blueberry?

4. How much chocolate cream, mincemeat, and cherry pie is there altogether?

Solve each problem.

Todd collects train cars. He has 42 train cars. One-third of the train cars are coal cars. How many coal cars does Todd have?

$$42 \times \frac{1}{3} = \frac{42}{3} \text{ or } 14 \text{ coal cars}$$

---

1. Chelsea has 32 marbles. If $\frac{1}{4}$ of the marbles are red, how many red marbles does she have?

2. Nicole has 60 marbles. One-third of Nicole's marbles are green, and $\frac{1}{6}$ of them are blue. How many green and blue marbles does Nicole have altogether?

3. Chad had 45 marbles. He lost $\frac{2}{9}$ of them to Travis and $\frac{1}{3}$ of them to Tua. How many marbles does Chad have left?

4. McKenzie has 21 marbles. Three-sevenths of her marbles are purple, and $\frac{1}{3}$ are silver. The rest of the marbles are orange. How many orange marbles does McKenzie have?

Solve each problem.

1. Jamie owes $360.00 to Tua's Famous Furniture. If she pays $\frac{1}{3}$ of the bill this month, how much will she still owe?

2. Jedd bought a new big-screen television. He paid for $\frac{1}{4}$ of the television when he ordered it. If he paid $1,283.12 when he ordered it, how much does he still owe?

3. Shannon wants to buy a new minivan. She has $4,283.92 saved, which will pay for $\frac{1}{5}$ of the van. How much does the van cost?

4. Sammy has $8.92 in her piggy bank. She wants to buy a pretty pony. She has $\frac{1}{3}$ of the amount she needs for the pretty pony. How much more money does Sammy need?

34

Solve each problem.

James eats 170 jars of baby food in one month. Forty percent of the food he eats is vegetables. How many jars of vegetables does James eat in one month?

170 x .40 = 68 jars of vegetables

1. James ate 14 jars of baby food. He ate $\frac{1}{7}$ of the baby food each day. How many jars of baby food did James eat each day?

2. It cost $37.92 to feed James for a week. How much did it cost to feed James each day?

3. James ate $\frac{3}{4}$ of a jar of green beans. What percentage of the green beans did he eat?

4. James used 40% of the diapers in the package. Write a fraction to show how many diapers James has used.

Solve each problem.

Marilyn is making copies for her nutrition class. There are 24 students in her class. Today 25% of the students will be absent. How many students will be in Marilyn's class?

$$
\begin{array}{r}
24 \\
\times\ .25 \\
\hline
6.00 \text{ absent}
\end{array}
\qquad
\begin{array}{r}
24 \\
-\ 6 \\
\hline
18 \text{ students in class}
\end{array}
$$

---

1. Kirsten and Katie are teaching a class on nutrition. The class lasts 50 minutes. Kirsten takes up 60% of the time. How many minutes are left for Katie?

2. Diane has 2 hours and 40 minutes to teach 4 classes. If each class is divided evenly, how many minutes are there in each class?

3. Susan teaches second grade for 6 hours. Math is 90 minutes. What percentage of the day does Susan spend teaching math?

4. Margaret spends 25% of her day teaching reading. She teaches for 6 hours. How much time does Margaret spend teaching reading?

Farmer Fred

Solve each problem.

1. Farmer Fred has 1,580 animals on his farm. Thirty percent of the animals are pigs. How many pigs does Farmer Fred have?

2. The chickens on Farmer Fred's farm lay 2,340 eggs each week. They lay 20% of the eggs on Tuesday and 35% of the eggs on Thursday. How many eggs do they lay on Tuesday and Thursday altogether?

3. Farmer Fred paid $3,278.00 for feed last month. It cost him 65% of the $3,278.00 to feed the cows. How much did it cost Farmer Fred to feed the cows last month?

4. Farmer Fred has 983 cows, 482 chickens, 86 horses, 127 sheep, and 75 goats. What percentage of Farmer Fred's animals are horses?

Solve each problem.

Conner waters his lawn 3 times per week for 40 minutes each time.
What percentage of the week does Conner water his lawn?
He waters 120 minutes per week (3 x 40).
The total number of minutes in a week is 24 x 60 x 7 = 10,080 minutes.
To get the percentage, divide the amount of time he waters (120) by
the total amount of time (10,080), which equals .0119 or **just over 1%.**

---

1. Bill likes to have a nice lawn. He waters 4 times per week for 35 minutes each time. What percentage of the week does he spend watering his lawn?

2. Rachel works in a pet shop. She spends 35% of her time at her store. How many hours does Rachel spend at her store each week?

3. The Lovely Lawn Service made $5,329.00 last month. Twenty-four percent of that amount went to taxes. How much did Lovely Lawn Service pay in taxes last month?

4. Grayson makes $20.00 for each lawn he mows. He mowed 26 lawns last month. Four percent of what he makes goes for gas. How much did Grayson have after he paid for his gas?

Solve each problem.

1. The Just Joking Joke Shop earned $1,563.30 this week. Twenty-three percent went to taxes, and 31% was paid to employees. How much did the joke shop make after paying their taxes and employees?

2. Forty-two percent of the items sold at the Just Joking Joke Shop were magic kits. The shop sold 543 items in the first week of March, 375 the second week, 647 the third week, and 535 the fourth week. How many magic kits did they sell in March?

3. The Just Joking Joke Shop has 732 masks, 275 rubber chickens, and 621 joke kits. They have 6 times as many trick books as rubber chickens. How many trick books, masks, and joke kits do they have altogether?

4. Just Joking Joke Shop sells 9 times more joke kits than bottles of invisible ink. They sell 621 joke kits. How many bottles of invisible ink do they sell?

Solve each problem. Remember to line the decimal points up before adding and subtracting.

Ze's Zoo bought food for the animals. They spent $532.82 on the lions, $872.29 on the tigers, $781.92 on the bears, and $1,284.72 on the camels. How much money did Ze's Zoo spend?	$ 532.82 $ 872.29 $ 781.92 + $1,284.72 $3,471.75

1. Ze's Zoo received their monthly feed bill. They spent $532.81 on the monkeys, $782.19 on the birds, $935.17 on the alligators, and $2,394.14 on the elephants. How much was Ze's Zoo's feed bill?

2. Ze has fed 72% of the animals. There are 200 animals in the zoo. How many animals does Ze still need to feed?

3. Emilee took her family to the zoo. It cost $4.50 for each person to get in. She paid for 7 people and gave the clerk $50.00. How much change will Emilee get?

4. Steve bought lunch for everyone. He bought 3 hot dogs for $1.49 each, 5 orders of fries for $1.19 each, 7 large drinks for $1.25 each, and 4 hamburgers for $2.20 each. How much did Steve spend?

Solve each problem.

(*M = made; A = attempted)

Basketball Game Summary						
	Minutes	Field Goals	Free Throws	Rebounds	Assists	Points
Lori	33	4–7 M–A*	2–4 M–A*	8	2	10
Grayson	29	3–5	1–2	4	5	7
Mike	31	5–8	2–2	5	3	12
Robert	22	1–3	1–1	2	2	3
Paul	25	2–4	3–3	3	1	7

1. What percentage of field goals did Mike make?

2. What is the team's field goal percentage?

3. What is the team's free throw percentage?

4. How many rebounds did Mike, Robert, and Paul have altogether?

41

Place Value
thousands hundreds tens ones . tenths hundredths thousandths

1. Lexie drives 22.3 miles each way traveling to and from work. She works 5 days per week. How many miles does Lexie travel in 4 weeks?

2. In 2003, 12.3 percent of people in Hurricane bought sports cars. That same year 23.6 percent bought trucks and 15.3 percent bought midsize cars. What is the total percentage of people that bought sports cars, trucks, and midsize cars?

3. Alissa took a trip. She traveled 354.3 miles on Thursday, 235.8 miles on Friday, and 269.1 miles on Saturday. How many miles did Alissa travel?

4. Max traveled twenty-three and four-tenths miles on Monday. He traveled fifty-seven and thirty-five thousandths miles on Tuesday and forty-nine and twenty-five hundredths miles on Wednesday. How many miles did Max travel altogether?

Take a Hike

Solve each problem.

> 5,280 feet = 1 mile 3 feet = 1 yard
>
> 36 inches = 1 yard 12 inches = 1 foot
>
> When converting a larger unit to a smaller unit (feet to inches), you multiply.
> When converting a smaller unit to a larger unit (inches to feet), you divide.
> Emilee walked $\frac{3}{4}$ of a mile. How many <u>feet</u> did she walk?
>
> $\frac{3}{4}$ x 5,280 = $\frac{3}{4}$ x $\frac{5280}{1}$ = 3 x 5,280 ÷ 4 = 3,960 feet

1. Kim hiked $\frac{1}{2}$ a mile. How many <u>feet</u> did Kim hike?

2. Tanner needs 168 inches of tape for his paint project. How many <u>feet</u> of tape should he buy?

3. Moises loves trains. One of his train tracks is 78 feet long. The other train track is 64 feet long. How many <u>yards</u> of train track does Moises have?

4. Allie's bike trail forms a triangle. One side is 56 yards long, the second side is 114 feet long, and the third side is 5,346 inches long. How many <u>feet</u> long is Allie's bike trail?

A **parallelogram** has four sides. Its opposite sides are parallel and equal. The **perimeter** is the distance around the outside of a figure.

Dan's house is a parallelogram. It is 11 yards long by 7 yards wide. What is the perimeter of Dan's house in feet?

11 yards + 11 yards + 7 yards + 7 yards =
36 yards x 3 (3 feet in each yard) = 108 feet

---

1. Jennifer has 3 rooms in her house. They are all parallelograms. The first is 6 feet 8 inches by 4 feet 5 inches. The second is 4 feet 2 inches by 4 feet 2 inches. The third is 5 feet 3 inches by 6 feet 2 in. What is the perimeter of all three rooms?

2. Sarah is 5 feet 4 inches tall. Jimmy is 5 feet 9 inches tall. Matt is 4 feet 3 inches tall. How tall are Sarah, Jimmy, and Matt altogether?

3. Rob is putting cupboards in his kitchen. The perimeter of his cupboards is shown.

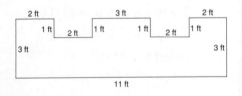

What is the perimeter of Rob's cupboards?

4. Matt's driveway is 10 yards long. His family's motor home is 183 inches long, and their boat is 8 feet 4 inches long. How long are the motor home and boat? Will they both fit in the driveway?

Equilateral means that all sides are the same or equal.

1. Marni had a board that was 6 feet long. She sawed off 42 inches. How many inches is Marni's board now?

2. Dalton's garden is an equilateral triangle, and one side is 23 feet long. He wants to buy red bricks to go around his garden. Each brick is 18 inches long. How many bricks does Dalton need?

3. Alexandria is putting fringe all the way around the gym for prom. The gym is a rectangle. It measures 20 yards by 14 yards. Each package of fringe is 8 feet long. How many packages does Alexandria need?

4. Dylan is building a fence around the pasture. One side is 359 yards 2 feet 7 inches. The second side is 195 yards 1 foot 8 inches. The third is 358 yards 1 foot 4 inches. The last side is 200 yards 2 feet 3 inches. How many yards is it around Dylan's pasture?

Word Problems Grade 6—RBP0784

Metric Measure

kilometer	hectometer	decameter	meter	decimeter	centimeter	millimeter
km	hm	dam	m	dm	cm	mm
1,000 m	100 m	10 m	1 m	1/10 m	1/100 m	1/1,000 m

Linda is putting bricks around her yard, which is 15 m by 11 m. Each brick is 15 cm long. How many bricks does she need?

15 + 15 + 11 + 11 = 52 m
52 meters = 5,200 cm
5,200 divided by 15 = 346.67
She needs 347 bricks.

---

1. Lori is putting tile around her swimming pool. Her pool is 18 meters by 12 meters. If each tile measures 2 decimeters, how many tiles does Lori need to go all the way around her pool?

2. Denise is making a quilt. The quilt measures 283 centimeters by 198 centimeters. What is the perimeter of the quilt in meters?

3. Fernando went on a trip last summer. He traveled 824 hectometers on Friday, 341 kilometers on Saturday, 4,329 decameters on Monday, and 28,731 meters on Tuesday. How many kilometers did he travel?

4. Rachel buys 30 decimeters of red fabric, 4 meters of pink fabric, 358 centimeters of white fabric, and 4,829 millimeters of yellow fabric. How many centimeters of fabric does Rachel have altogether?

Solve each problem.

1. Jedd is on the track team. He runs 3.2 kilometers, does four 200m sprints, six 100m sprints, and two 400m races each day. How many kilometers does he run in 6 days?

2. The total perimeter of Rachel's yard measures 64 meters. If each side is equivalent, how many meters is one side?

3. Shannon is making cards that are 120 millimeters by 180 millimeters. She needs to order envelopes for the cards. The length and width each need to be 1 centimeter larger than the card. How many centimeters long and wide should the envelopes be?

4. Max is taking a trip. It is 439 kilometers from his house to Lewiston. It is 392 kilometers from Lewiston to Jamesville, and it is 743 kilometers from Jamesville to Smithfield. Max is going to Smithfield and back. How many kilometers will Max's trip be?

Ounce for Ounce

1 gallon = 4 quarts   1 quart = 2 pints
1 pint = 2 cups   1 cup = 8 ounces
1 tablespoon = 3 teaspoons

Jeanne is making mustard pickles. She makes 5 batches. Each batch makes 8 quarts. Jeanne puts the pickles in pint jars. How many pint jars will 5 batches make?

5 batches x 8 quarts = 40 quarts
40 quarts x 2 = 80 pints

1. J'lene needs 24 quarts of punch for a party. The punch she wants is sold in gallon bottles and costs $3.49 per gallon. How much will the punch cost?

2. Sandra is making a cheese-cake. Her recipe calls for 2 tablespoons and 2 tea-spoons of vanilla. She can only find the $\frac{1}{2}$-teaspoon to measure with. How many half-teaspoons of vanilla does Sandra need?

3. Rex is making hot chocolate. In one batch he makes 64 cups, and in another batch he makes 52 cups. If he puts the hot chocolate in pint jars, how many jars will he need?

4. Boise High is having a bake sale to raise money. Chad is making brownies for the sale. Each batch calls for 64 ounces of chocolate chips. How many cups of chocolate chips will Chad need to make 3 batches?

Solve each problem.

1. Lori is making her grand-mother's recipe for yams. The recipe says to use two 64-ounce cans of yams. The only yams Lori could find at the store were in 20-ounce cans. How many 20-ounce cans should Lori buy?

2. Brandy is making gravy for Thanksgiving dinner. One package of gravy mix makes 2 cups. Brandy wants to make 3 quarts of gravy. How many packages of gravy mix will Brandy need?

3. Jeanne is making 2 pumpkin pies. Each pie recipe calls for 2 cups of pumpkin. The pumpkin comes in 20-ounce cans. How many cans should Jeanne buy?

4. Mike is making punch for Thanksgiving dinner. There are 17 people coming to dinner. Mike thinks each person will drink 3 cups of punch. How many quarts of punch should Mike make if each person drinks 3 cups?

Solve each problem.

1. One can of soda pop is 8 ounces. George drinks 32 ounces of soda pop every day for a week. How many 8-ounce cans of soda pop does George drink in a week?

2. A 2-liter bottle of soda pop holds 2.1 quarts. How many ounces are in a 2-liter bottle of soda pop?

3. Two gallons of apple juice is equal to how many cups?

4. Ninety-six pints of oil is equal to how many gallons?

1 ton = 2,000 pounds   1 pound = 16 ounces

Josh hauls 6 $\frac{1}{2}$ tons of dirt to the dump.
How many pounds of dirt does Josh haul
to the dump?

$$\begin{array}{r} 2{,}000 \\ \times\ 6.5 \\ \hline \mathbf{13{,}000}\ \textbf{pounds} \end{array}$$

---

1. If one potato weighs 10 ounces, about how many potatoes are in a 10-pound bag?

2. One bag of M&M's weighs 14.5 ounces. If each individually wrapped package in the bag weighs half an ounce, how many individually wrapped packages of M&M's are in the bag?

3. The car dealer sells three quarter-ton trucks. How many pounds are in three-quarters of a ton?

4. Carl's Apple Service picked 457 pounds of apples. How many ounces does 457 pounds weigh?

Solve each problem.

1. The Dirty Dirt Company hauls 3,456 tons of dirt a day. Each truck can haul 356 tons. How many loads will it take to haul the 3,456 tons of dirt?

2. The Dirty Dirt Company is donating the dirt for sandboxes at 125 elementary schools. Each sandbox holds 1,600 ounces of dirt. How many pounds of dirt is the Dirty Dirt Company donating?

3. Mike is building a new home. He hires the Dirty Dirt Company to haul off the extra dirt. He pays them $132 for every ton of dirt they haul. Dirty Dirt hauls off 7 loads. Each load weighs 1,000 pounds. How much does Mike owe Dirty Dirt Company?

4. Grayson is putting in a garden. He buys eighteen bags of topsoil. Each bag weighs 50 pounds. If the topsoil costs $1.13 per pound, how much did Grayson pay for topsoil?

Degrees are units used to measure angles. There are **360 degrees** in a **circle**.

If all the slices in a round pizza are cut at 12-degree angles, how many slices are in a whole pizza?

360 ÷ 12 = 30 slices

---

1. If all the slices in a pizza are cut at a 45-degree angle, how many slices are there in a whole pizza?

2. If 2 slices of pizza are cut at 45-degree angles, 1 slice is cut at a 90-degree angle, and 2 slices are cut at 20-degree angles, how many degrees of the pizza were cut?

3. If 1 whole pizza is cut into 20-degree angles, and the second pizza is cut into 30-degree angles, how many slices are there in both pizzas?

4. George eats one-third of the pizza. How many degrees of the pizza is one-third equal to?

53

Right angle: an angle that is exactly 90 degrees
Acute angle: an angle that is less than 90 degrees
Straight angle: an angle that is exactly 180 degrees
Obtuse angle: an angle that is more than 90 degrees, but less
than 180 degrees

1. If Rob cuts a circle in half, what type of an angle does he have?

2. Emilee cuts a circle so that all the pieces have a right angle. How many pieces will she get from 1 circle?

3. If Margaret wants to cut a board at a 60-degree angle, and the board is 100 degrees to start with, how many degrees does Margaret need to cut from the board?

4. Diane cuts out $\frac{1}{8}$ of a circle. What type of an angle did Diane cut out?

©RBP Books

To find the area of a triangle, multiply $\frac{1}{2}$ of the base times the height. Express your answer in terms of square units.

Area of a triangle = $\frac{1}{2}$ (B x H)

The floor of Shep's doghouse is triangular. Steve wants to put new carpet on the floor. The base is 15 inches, and the height is 20 inches. What is the area of the floor in Shep's doghouse?

$\frac{1}{2}$ (15 x 20) = $\frac{1}{2}$ x 300 = $\frac{300}{2}$

300 ÷ 2 = 150 square inches

---

1. Rachel wants to put new carpet in her craft room. The room is triangular. The room is 6 feet long by 8 feet wide at the base. How many square feet of carpet does Rachel need to order?

2. Emilee is putting wallpaper in a triangular shape on half of her bedroom wall. The area has a base of 7 feet and a height of 9 feet. How many square feet of wallpaper does she need?

3. Rob is building a greenhouse. The front is a triangle. The base is 12 feet, and the height is 16 feet. Siding to go on the front costs $5.69 per square foot. How much will siding cost Rob?

4. Matt is putting a garden in his yard. The garden will be a triangle. One side is 38 feet long (height), and the other is 24 feet long (base). How many square feet will Matt's garden be?

Word Problems Grade 6—RBP0784

Silly Circumference

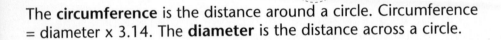

The **circumference** is the distance around a circle. Circumference = diameter x 3.14. The **diameter** is the distance across a circle.

Grayson wants to put a fence around his circular garden. The distance across his garden is 18 feet. What is the distance around Grayson's garden?

diameter x 3.14

18 x 3.14 = 56.52 feet

1. Brandon wants to put a rock edge around his circular driveway. The distance across his driveway is 22 feet. What is the circumference (distance around) of Brandon's driveway?

2. Carol is making fluffy snowmen with circles of fleece. The circles are 12 inches across. She wants to put lace around each circle. How much lace will Carol need to go around 4 circles?

3. Brent is painting a circular logo on his company truck. He is putting a chrome decal around the logo. The logo is $8\frac{1}{2}$ inches across. How much chrome decal does Brent need to buy to go around the logo?

4. Quentin's school has a circular library that is 10 yards across. His class is putting a paper chain all the way around the room. How many feet of chain does Quentin's class need to make?

Solve each problem.

1. Lori is making a cloth snowman. She cuts out a circular piece of material. The piece has a diameter of 14 inches. How many inches around is Lori's cloth circle?

2. Emilee is putting in a circular flower bed. She is putting edging around the flower bed. The flower bed has a diameter of 18 feet. How many feet of edging does Emilee need to buy?

3. Rachel is making a circular quilt. She wants to put lace around the quilt. The quilt is 36 inches across. How many inches of lace does Rachel need to buy?

4. Grayson cuts a piece of wood into a circle. The wood circle is 3 feet 6 inches across. How many inches around is his wood circle?

57

To find the **area** of a circle, multiply the radius times the radius times 3.14. Express your answer in square units.
The **radius** is half of the distance across a circle.
Area of a circle = r^2 x 3.14

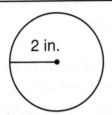

2 in.

A = (2 x 2) x 3.14

4 x 3.14 = 12.56 in.²

---

1. Dave is putting a circular cement pad in his yard. The distance across the circle is 16 feet (Remember: the radius is half the distance across a circle). How many square feet of cement does Dave need to order?

2. Denise has a circular flower bed. She wants to buy ground cover and needs to know how many square feet she needs. The radius of the flower bed is 10 feet. How many square feet are there in Denise's flower bed?

3. Matt is putting wood chips in his circular window box. The distance across the window box is 26 inches. How many square inches are in Matt's window box?

4. Rob is putting a new cover on his circular swimming pool. The pool is 24 feet across. How many square feet are in Rob's circular swimming pool cover?

A **ratio** is a comparison of 2 numbers. The numbers in the ratio are separated with a colon (:) or written as a fraction. The ratio of 2 and 5 can be written 2:5 or 2/5, and we say the ratio is 2 to 5.

In Allie's class the ratio is 2 boys to 1 girl. There are 21 students in Allie's class. How many of those students are girls?

To find the number of girls in the class, add the numbers in the ratio together (2 + 1 = 3) and divide the sum (3) into the number of students in the class. The quotient is the answer you get. Multiply the quotient times the number from the ratio you are looking for to get your answer.

21 students ÷ 3 = 7
7 (the quotient) x 1 (number from the ratio) = 7 girls in Allie's class

1. In Allie's class the ratio is 3 boys to 1 girl. There are 36 students in Allie's class. How many are boys?

2. In Lori's class the ratio is 3 boys to 2 girls. There are 35 students in Lori's class. How many are girls?

3. In Denise's class the ratio is 2 girls to 1 boy. There are 18 students in Denise's class. How many are boys?

4. In Emilee's class the ratio is 5 girls to 2 boys. There are 21 students in Emilee's class. How many are girls?

Word Problems Grade 6—RBP0784

Mike is balancing his checkbook. His beginning balance is $983.27.

1. Mike had $983.27 in his checking account. He writes 3 checks. The first is for $46.29. The second is for $382.10, and the third is for $82.20. How much money does Mike have in his checking account now?

2. Mike had $472.68 in his checking account. He makes a deposit for $1,565.29 and a deposit for $50.00. He writes a check for $68.29. How much money does Mike have in his checking account?

3. Mike had $3,582.61 in his savings account. He got 3.2% interest on that amount of money. After adding the interest, how much money does Mike have in his savings account?

4. Mike had $2,019.68 in his checking account. He writes checks for $43.29, $901.82, $56.10, and $18.73. He makes a deposit for $100.00, and he transfers $200.00 out of checking into savings. How much money does Mike now have in his checking account?

Estimate how much James will spend. When estimating, round to the nearest dollar.

James went to the grocery store and bought milk for $2.79, bread for $1.19, juice for $3.10, and butter for $.89. About how much did James spend?	$3 $1 $3 + $1 $8.00	James spent about $8.00

1. At the pet store, James bought cat food for $6.99, cat litter for $3.17, a cat collar for $4.89, and a cat toy for $2.38. About how much money did James spend at the pet store?

2. At the mall James bought a shirt for $17.99, a jacket for $59.99, and a pair of pants for $29.89. About how much did James spend?

3. For a science project James bought a poster board for $1.19, markers for $3.89, vinegar for $1.25, baking soda for $1.89, and clay for $4.97. About how much money did James spend?

4. James bought toothpaste for $3.99, a toothbrush for $1.89, dental floss for $4.87, a comb for $.97, a hairbrush for $2.29, and lotion for $3.39. About how much did James spend?

Word Problems Grade 6—RBP0784

Estimate How Much Was Spent

Solve each problem. Estimate to the nearest dollar.

1. Linda went to the movies. She spent $8.00 to get in. She spent $3.89 on popcorn, $2.75 on a drink, and $2.25 on candy. About how much did Linda spend at the movies?

2. Last month Jimmy spent $35.50 to go golfing, $26.17 at the movies, $56.29 on a video game, and $119.82 at the arcade. About how much did Jimmy spend?

3. Estimate the total cost of the following: $4.89, $2.57, $6.98, $.24, $2.19, $5.78, $4.21, $1.29.

4. Estimate the total cost of the following: $29.99, $123.02, $47.32, $16.12, $43.78, $2.26, $74.89, $257.16.

Guess and Check

Solve each problem.

1. Connie has 7 coins that total $.48. What coins does Connie have?

2. Jamie left a message for McKenzie on a page in her math book. There are 155 pages in the book. The page number is a 3-digit number. One of the digits is a 4, and the total of all 3 digits in the page number is 11. On what page is the message?

3. Mike drove to see a friend. He drove more than 150 miles, but less than 220 miles. The number of miles he drove is divisible by 5 and by 9. How many miles did Mike drive?

4. A road has 6 houses in a row. Read the clues and list the order of the houses.
A. Mark's house is to the left of Jeanne's and Brent's houses.
B. Jeanne's and Lyndon's houses are on the ends.
C. Dylan's and Brent's houses are in the middle.
D. Alexandria's house is between Brent's and Jeanne's houses.

Word Problems Grade 6—RBP0784

Paul's Pizza

Solve each problem.

Paul's Pizza

Cheese.......$7.99	Pepperoni.....$8.99
Combo.......$9.99	Hawaiian.......$9.99
Bread Sticks....$3.49	Hot Wings......$2.99

1. Denise ordered pizza for her birthday party. She ordered 1 cheese pizza, 2 combo pizzas, and 2 pepperoni pizzas. She also got 2 orders of bread sticks. She gave the delivery boy a $5.00 tip. How much did Denise spend?

2. North Star Elementary is selling pizzas for $11.99 each. North Star gets $4.50 for each pizza sold. They sell 45 pizzas on Monday, 32 on Tuesday, 43 on Wednesday, 27 on Thursday, and 67 on Friday. How much did North Star make?

3. Sheri is ordering pizza for her company party. A large pizza has 12 slices. Sheri is estimating 50 people will come. She thinks each person will eat 2 pieces. How many large pizzas should Sheri order?

4. Joanne orders pizza for her family party. She orders 3 combo pizzas, 4 cheese pizzas, 3 pepperoni pizzas, 5 orders of bread sticks, and 4 orders of hot wings. How much will this cost Joanne?

Equal

Write what the following amounts or lengths are equal to.

> 317 weeks is equal to how many years?
>
> **317 ÷ 52 = 6 years and 5 weeks**

---

1. One dozen eggs costs $.79. How much will 7 dozen eggs cost?

2. Eighteen weeks is equal to how many days?

---

3. Twenty-three quarters is equal to how much money?

4. Twenty-four yards is equal to how many feet?

© RBP Books   Word Problems Grade 6—RBP0784

What Do You Think?

Solve each problem.

1. Joe is a caterer. One hundred forty-five people are coming for a business party. He has 6 dozen dinners ready. How many more dinners does Joe need to make for the party?

2. Grayson can build a fire with 6 twigs of wood. George uses 8 times as many twigs as Grayson. How many twigs does George use to build a fire?

3. Nancy has 16 gardens. She grows 6 kinds of flowers in half of each of the gardens and 11 kinds of flowers in the other half of each garden. How many kinds of flowers does Nancy grow?

4. Myrna has 35 vases. She puts 3 flowers in each vase. How many flowers does she have?

Anniversary Party

Solve each problem.

1. Slip and Slide Ski Resort sold 456 passes on Thursday, 583 passes on Friday, and 782 passes on Saturday. Passes cost $24.50 each. How much money did they make on the three days altogether?

2. Jenneil is putting new carpet in two rooms. She finds a remnant that will fit one room. It costs $36.72. The second room is 12 feet by 14 feet. The carpet for this room costs $7.50 per square foot. How much does Jenneil spend on carpet?

3. Ellie is baking cookies to give to her neighbors. She bakes 3 batches on Monday, 5 batches on Tuesday, 2 batches on Wednesday, 4 batches on Thursday, and 7 batches on Friday. Each batch makes a dozen and a half. How many cookies did Ellie bake this week?

4. Brent is planning a dinner for his parents' 50th wedding anniversary. He has invited 120 people. He is planning on 70% of the people coming. Each dinner costs $15.90. How much will it cost Brent if 70% of the people come?

Solve each problem.

1. Brandon went to the ocean aquarium while he was on vacation. He saw 183 angelfish and 52 starfish. If Brandon saw 5 times as many clown fish as starfish, how many fish did Brandon see altogether?

2. KayCee bought a new outfit at Quentin's Dress Shop. She spent $143.50 on a dress, $65.90 on shoes, $4.99 on nylons, and $69.90 on a necklace. Sales tax is 5.5%. How much did KayCee's new outfit cost?

3. The Sports Mart made $987.21 the week before New Year's. Fifty-six percent of this amount went for expenses. How much money did Sports Mart pay in expenses that week?

4. It snowed 84 inches at the Slip and Slide Ski Resort last week. This is 30% of their average annual snow-fall. On average, how much snow does the Slip and Slide Ski Resort receive during the year?

Solve each problem.

The library is 538 feet tall. The bank is 436 feet tall. How much taller is the library than the bank?

$$\begin{array}{r} 538 \\ -\ 436 \\ \hline \textbf{102 feet} \end{array}$$

---

1. The mall is 917 feet tall. The utility company's building is 542 feet tall. How much taller is the mall than the utility company's building?

2. Rob wants new carpet for his bedroom. His room is 18 feet by 24 feet. How many square feet of carpet will Rob need?

3. Lori went on a trip. Her flight took 3 hours and 10 minutes. Next week she is flying 4 times as far. How long is she flying next week?

4. Marni is making applesauce. She bought 17 boxes of apples. Each box cost $14.50. How much did Marni spend on apples?

Solve each problem.

Jamie buys 56 apples. She cuts the apples into thirds. How many slices does she have?

$$56$$
$$\times\ \ 3$$
168 slices

---

1. Grayson buys 6 dozen donuts for $4.99 per dozen. He buys 3 gallons of punch for $1.49 per gallon. He buys 1 package of cups for $3.59 and 1 package of napkins for $.89. How much money does Grayson spend?

2. Rachel buys 49 apples. If she cuts them into fourths, how many slices will she have?

3. Lyndon cut a pie into eighths. If three-fourths of the pie has been eaten, how many slices of pie are left?

4. Maggie is painting 3 rooms in her house. She bought 4 gallons of paint for each room. Each gallon cost her $15.99. How much did Maggie spend on paint?

Solve each problem.

Susan is making cookies. She is going to double the recipe. The recipe asks for $2\frac{3}{4}$ cups of sugar. How much sugar will Susan need to double the recipe?

$$2\frac{3}{4} \times 2 = \frac{11}{4} \times \frac{2}{1} = \frac{22}{4} \text{ or } 5\frac{1}{2} \text{ cups of sugar}$$

1. Brandon worked at a fruit stand. He sold 96 boxes of fruit. Twenty-five percent of the fruit sold was apples. How many boxes of apples did Brandon sell?

2. Allie collected 34 geodes. The geodes make up 10% of her rock collection. How many rocks does Allie have altogether?

3. Stevane is making 3 cakes for a New Year's party. It takes $4\frac{1}{3}$ cups of flour to make one cake. How much flour does Stevane need to make all 3 cakes?

4. Tanner is making cookies. He needs to triple the recipe to have enough cookies. The recipe asks for $3\frac{1}{2}$ cups of sugar. How much sugar does Tanner need to triple his cookie recipe?

Solve each problem.

Joanne has 351 books. Two-ninths of her books are historical fiction novels. How many historical fiction novels does Joanne have?

$$351 \times \frac{2}{9} = \frac{702}{9} \text{ or 78 historical fiction novels}$$

1. Tua has 35 video games. He got $\frac{1}{7}$ of those games for his birthday. How many video games did Tua get for his birthday?

2. Dylan has 172 chickens. Twenty-five percent of his chickens are guinea hens. How many guinea hens does Dylan have?

3. Ze's Zoo buys food weekly for its animals. They spend $492.92 on the lions, $729.39 on the tigers, $1,208.92 on the bears, and $274.29 on the monkeys. How much does Ze's Zoo spend on food each week?

4. Marni is putting a fence around her yard. Her yard is a parallelogram that is 37 feet by 29 feet. What is the perimeter of her yard?

Solve each problem.

Mom is making 7 batches of peanut brittle. She needs 21 ounces of corn syrup for one batch. There are 25 ounces in each bottle of corn syrup. How many bottles does Mom need to buy?
7 x 21 = 147 ounces in 7 batches. 147 ÷ 25 ounces per bottle = 5.88. She needs to buy 6 bottles of corn syrup.

---

1. Ellie is making caramels. She needs 42 ounces of sweetened condensed milk for 3 batches. There are 14 ounces in one can of milk. How many cans will Ellie need to buy?

2. KayCee has four half-circles. How many degrees are in one half-circle?

3. George wants to cut his circle into pieces so that each piece has a right angle. How many pieces should George cut his circle into?

4. In Diane's class the ratio is 2 girls to 1 boy. There are 27 students in Diane's class. How many of those students are girls?

Solve each problem.

1. Quentin had $235.29 in his checking account. He makes two deposits. One is for $136.72, and the other is for $371.29. He writes three checks. The first check is for $43.27, the second is for $82.12, and the third is for $72.18. How much money does Quentin have in his checking account now?

2. James went to the video store. He rented two movies for $2.75 each. He bought a used DVD for $9.99 and a new video game for $43.29. He bought popcorn for $1.89 and drinks for $2.88. Estimate how much James spent at the video store.

3. Connie has 34 cents. She has 7 coins. What coins does Connie have?

4. Fifty-one feet is equal to how many yards?

Answer Pages

Page 3
1. $2.10
2. 65 minutes
3. $58.12
4. No. He has $79.57.

Page 4
1. 8 packs
2. 135 balls
3. 21.3 points
4. 9.25 rebounds

Page 5
1. 24.8 inches
2. 7,920 feet
3. 2,640 chairs
4. $87,093.60

Page 6
1. 109 inches
2. 20 baseboards
3. $21.80
4. $2,023.90

Page 7
1. 3 dozen
2. $147.15
3. 316 pounds
4. $166.75

Page 8
1. 3,399 pets
2. 483 birds
3. $9,427.59
4. $3,686.63

Page 9
1. 992 animals
2. 342 bales of straw
3. 294 more eggs
4. 43 dozen

Page 10
1. 62%
2. 33.8%
3. No
4. 282 votes

Page 11
1. $43.00
2. $36.39
3. $72.00
4. $58.28

Page 12
1. 7 cups flour
   $\frac{1}{2}$ cup sugar
   1 teaspoon salt
   $1\frac{3}{4}$ teaspoons baking powder
2. 4 slices
3. 1 pound 11 ounces
4. $461.60

Page 13
1. $193.15
2. 443 more T-shirts
3. 593 pieces of equipment
4. 90 snowboards

Page 14
1. 14.42 inches
2. 43.25 inches
3. 24.7 inches
4. 2,177 feet taller

Answer Pages

Page 15
1. 379 feet
2. 1,614 feet
3. $2,699,478 more
4. $47,311.32

Page 16
1. $224.57
2. $3,359.61
3. $176.69
4. $92,498.96

Page 17
1. 877 square feet
2. $1,575.84
3. 87,492 nails
4. 13.5 sheets

Page 18
1. 162.54 gallons
2. $443.87
3. 22 chocolate ice cream cones
4. 34 gallons

Page 19
1. 328 softballs
2. 8 hours 15 minutes
3. 26.45 bushels
4. $996.00

Page 20
1. $25.69
2. $50.93
3. 23 pies, 5 apples left over
4. 261 slices

Page 21
1. 147 diapers
2. $134.61
3. 2.33 or $2\frac{1}{3}$ mega packs
4. $81.00

Page 22
1. 17%
2. 14.5%
3. 67%
4. $\frac{8}{100}$ or $\frac{2}{25}$

Page 23
1. $171\frac{1}{2}$ hours
2. $11.99
3. $410.49
4. $738.69

Page 24
1. 372 bags, 14 apples left over
2. 126 bushels of apples
3. 22 boxes
4. 211 apple trees

Page 25
1. 310 igneous and metamorphic rocks
2. $15.80
3. 160.38 rocks
4. 31 rooms

Page 26
1. 553 minutes
2. $1.01
3. 124 baseballs
4. $38,033.04

Answer Pages

Page 27
1. 77 lengths
2. $301.12
3. 1,596 square feet
4. $179.01

Page 28
1. 2,906 flowers
2. 37 hours
3. 2,435 flowers
4. 473 trees

Page 29
1. $8 \frac{1}{2}$ cups of flour
2. 40 bags
3. $256.49
4. $2,772.63

Page 30
1. $19 \frac{1}{2}$ hours
2. $345.36
3. 16,618 gallons
4. $3,484.77

Page 31
1. $\frac{5}{8}$ teaspoon of garlic
2. $13 \frac{1}{2}$ cups of flour
3. $11 \frac{2}{3}$ cups of sugar
4. $20 \frac{5}{12}$ cups altogether

Page 32
1. $\frac{11}{12}$ of a pie
2. cherry pie
3. $\frac{1}{6}$ more apple pie
4. $\frac{19}{24}$ of a pie

Page 33
1. 8 red marbles
2. 30 green and blue marbles
3. 20 marbles
4. 5 orange marbles

Page 34
1. $240.00
2. $3,849.36
3. $21,419.60
4. $17.84 more

Page 35
1. 2 jars
2. $5.42
3. 75%
4. $\frac{40}{100}$ or $\frac{2}{5}$ of the diapers in the package

Page 36
1. 20 minutes
2. 40 minutes
3. 25%
4. $1\frac{1}{2}$ hours or 90 minutes

Page 37
1. 474 pigs
2. 1,287 eggs
3. $2,130.70
4. 4.9%

Page 38
1. 1.4%
2. 58.8 hours per week
3. $1,278.96
4. $499.20

Answer Pages

Page 39
1. $719.12
2. 882 magic kits
3. 3,003 altogether
4. 69 bottles of invisible ink

Page 40
1. $4,644.31
2. 56 animals
3. $18.50
4. $27.97

Page 41
1. 62.5%
2. 55.6%
3. 75%
4. 10 rebounds

Page 42
1. 892 miles
2. 51.2%
3. 859.2 miles
4. 129.685 miles

Page 43
1. 2,640 feet
2. 14 feet
3. 47 $\frac{1}{3}$ yards or 47 yards 1 foot
4. 727 $\frac{1}{2}$ feet or 727 feet 6 inches

Page 44
1. 61 feet 8 inches
2. 15 feet 4 inches
3. 32 feet
4. 283 inches, yes

Page 45
1. 30 inches
2. 46 bricks
3. 26 packages
4. 1,114 yards 1 foot 10 inches

Page 46
1. 300 tiles
2. 9.62 meters
3. 495.421 kilometers
4. 1,540.9 centimeters

Page 47
1. 5.4 kilometers
2. 16 meters
3. 13 centimeters by 19 centimeters
4. 3,148 kilometers

Page 48
1. $20.94
2. 16 half-teaspoons
3. 58 jars
4. 24 cups

Page 49
1. 7 cans
2. 6 packages
3. 2 cans
4. 13 quarts

Page 50
1. 28 cans
2. 67.2 ounces
3. 32 cups
4. 12 gallons

Answer Pages

Page 51
1. 16 potatoes
2. 29 packages
3. 1,500 pounds
4. 7,312 ounces

Page 52
1. 10 loads (9.70)
2. 12,500 pounds
3. $462.00
4. $1,017.00

Page 53
1. 8 slices
2. 220 degrees
3. 30 slices
4. 120 degrees

Page 54
1. straight angle or no angle
2. 4 pieces
3. 40 degrees
4. acute angle

Page 55
1. 24 square feet
2. $31\frac{1}{2}$ square feet
3. $546.24
4. 456 square feet

Page 56
1. 69.08 feet
2. 150.72 inches
3. 26.69 inches
4. 94.2 feet

Page 57
1. 43.96 inches
2. 56.52 feet
3. 113.04 inches
4. 131.88 inches

Page 58
1. 200.96 square feet
2. 314 square feet
3. 530.66 square inches
4. 452.16 square feet

Page 59
1. 27 boys
2. 14 girls
3. 6 boys
4. 15 girls

Page 60
1. $472.68
2. $2,019.68
3. $3,697.25
4. $899.74

Page 61
1. about $17.00
2. about $108.00
3. about $13.00
4. about $17.00

Page 62
1. about $17.00
2. about $238.00
3. about $28.00
4. about $594.00

Answer Pages

Page 63
1. 1 quarter, 1 dime, 2 nickels, 3 pennies
2. page 146
3. 180 miles
4. Lyndon, Mark, Dylan, Brent, Alexandria, Jeanne

Page 64
1. $57.93
2. $963.00
3. 9 pizzas
4. $118.31

Page 65
1. $5.53
2. 126 days
3. $5.75
4. 72 feet

Page 66
1. 73 dinners
2. 48 twigs
3. 136 flowers
4. 105 flowers

Page 67
1. $44,614.50
2. $1,296.72
3. 378 cookies
4. $1,335.60

Page 68
1. 495 fish
2. $299.93
3. $552.84
4. 280 inches

Page 69
1. 375 feet
2. 432 square feet
3. 12 hours 40 minutes
4. $246.50

Page 70
1. $38.89
2. 196 slices
3. 2 slices
4. $191.88

Page 71
1. 24 boxes
2. 340 rocks
3. 13 cups
4. 10 $\frac{1}{2}$ cups

Page 72
1. 5 video games
2. 43 guinea hens
3. $2,705.52
4. 132 feet

Page 73
1. 3 cans
2. 180 degrees
3. 4 pieces
4. 18 girls

Page 74
1. $545.73
2. about $64.00
3. 3 dimes, 4 pennies
4. 17 yards

Answer Pages

Page 63
1. 1 quarter, 1 dime, 2 nickels, 3 pennies
2. page 146
3. 180 miles
4. Lyndon, Mark, Dylan, Brent, Alexandria, Jeanne

Page 64
1. $57.93
2. $963.00
3. 9 pizzas
4. $118.31

Page 65
1. $5.53
2. 126 days
3. $5.75
4. 72 feet

Page 66
1. 73 dinners
2. 48 twigs
3. 136 flowers
4. 105 flowers

Page 67
1. $44,614.50
2. $1,296.72
3. 378 cookies
4. $1,335.60

Page 68
1. 495 fish
2. $299.93
3. $552.84
4. 280 inches

Page 69
1. 375 feet
2. 432 square feet
3. 12 hours 40 minutes
4. $246.50

Page 70
1. $38.89
2. 196 slices
3. 2 slices
4. $191.88

Page 71
1. 24 boxes
2. 340 rocks
3. 13 cups
4. 10 $\frac{1}{2}$ cups

Page 72
1. 5 video games
2. 43 guinea hens
3. $2,705.52
4. 132 feet

Page 73
1. 3 cans
2. 180 degrees
3. 4 pieces
4. 18 girls

Page 74
1. $545.73
2. about $64.00
3. 3 dimes, 4 pennies
4. 17 yards

Answer Pages

Page 51
1. 16 potatoes
2. 29 packages
3. 1,500 pounds
4. 7,312 ounces

Page 52
1. 10 loads (9.70)
2. 12,500 pounds
3. $462.00
4. $1,017.00

Page 53
1. 8 slices
2. 220 degrees
3. 30 slices
4. 120 degrees

Page 54
1. straight angle or no angle
2. 4 pieces
3. 40 degrees
4. acute angle

Page 55
1. 24 square feet
2. $31\frac{1}{2}$ square feet
3. $546.24
4. 456 square feet

Page 56
1. 69.08 feet
2. 150.72 inches
3. 26.69 inches
4. 94.2 feet

Page 57
1. 43.96 inches
2. 56.52 feet
3. 113.04 inches
4. 131.88 inches

Page 58
1. 200.96 square feet
2. 314 square feet
3. 530.66 square inches
4. 452.16 square feet

Page 59
1. 27 boys
2. 14 girls
3. 6 boys
4. 15 girls

Page 60
1. $472.68
2. $2,019.68
3. $3,697.25
4. $899.74

Page 61
1. about $17.00
2. about $108.00
3. about $13.00
4. about $17.00

Page 62
1. about $17.00
2. about $238.00
3. about $28.00
4. about $594.00

79